□ NATIONAL GEOGRAPHIC
my first pocket Guide

WEATHER

Consultant: Tom Kierein
Illustrators: Robert Cremins, Theophilus Britt Griswold,
Stuart Armstrong

Published by
The National Geographic Society
John M. Fahey, Jr., President and Chief Executive Officer
Gilbert M. Grosvenor, Chairman of the Board
Nina D. Hoffman, Executive Vice President,
President of Books and School Publishing
William R. Gray, Vice President and Director, Book Division

Staff for this Book
Barbara Brownell, Director of Continuities
Marianne R. Koszorus, Design Director
Toni Eugene, Editor
Alexandra Littlehales, Art Director
Patricia Daniels, Writer-Researcher
Susan V. Kelly, Illustrations Editor
Sharon Kocsis Berry, Illustrations Assistant
Mark A. Caraluzzi, Vice President, Sales and Marketing
Heidi Vincent, Director of Direct Response Marketing
Vincent P. Ryan, Manufacturing Manager
Lewis R. Bassford, Production Project Manager

Visit our Web site at www.nationalgeographic.com

Library of Congress Catalog Card Number: 99-70469
ISBN: 0-7922-3460-X
Trade Edition ISBN: 0-7922-6588-2

Color separations by Quad Graphics, Martinsburg, West Virginia
Printed in Mexico by R.R. Donnelley & Sons Company

NATIONAL GEOGRAPHIC

my first Pocket Guide

WEATHER

PATRICIA DANIELS

All photographs supplied by Animals Animals/Earth Scenes

INTRODUCTION

Everybody talks about the weather," writer Mark Twain supposedly joked, "but nobody *does* anything about it." It's true that people love to discuss—and watch—the weather. Weather is what the air around you is doing at this moment. Is it cold and windy? Hot and dry? Has warm, moist air formed thunderclouds? Unlike climate, which means the conditions a region experiences over many years, weather is constantly changing.

Our changeable weather can have serious effects. Droughts ruin farmers' crops. Blizzards send cars spiraling off the road. Hurricanes lay waste to entire countries. That's why it is so important to be able to predict the weather. Maybe we can't change it, but we can be prepared for it. That preparation can mean the difference between life and death.

Meteorologists, people who study weather, use satellites and computers to predict the weather for at least a few days ahead. You can use the oldest tools of all:

your eyes. By watching the skies and measuring wind and temperature, you can predict the weather, too.

HOW TO USE THIS BOOK

Weather occurs all over the world. This book focuses on North America and is organized by kinds of weather. The first section describes causes of weather. The one that follows explains how to identify particular kinds. Each spread gives facts about that weather's cause and place in the atmosphere. The "Forecast" box contains a weather's symbol and explains how to predict it. The "Field Notes" entry has some interesting facts about each kind of weather. If you see a word you don't know, look it up in the Glossary on page 76.

SUN, EARTH, AND AIR

Heat from the sun makes weather on Earth. This is because the planet heats up unevenly. The Earth is round and tilted in its orbit around the sun, so when one half cools off for winter, the other warms up for summer (see pages 8-9). It is always cold at the Poles and hot at the Equator. Land heats and cools quickly, while water holds heat much longer. The air over all these places is also warming up and cooling off, rising and falling, and moving

exosphere

thermosphere

mesosphere

stratosphere

troposphere

around Earth in a swirl of air masses.

Almost all this action occurs in the lowest level of the atmosphere, called the troposphere. The troposphere is a heavy, moist, cloudy layer of air that extends about six to ten miles above Earth's surface. Beyond the troposphere are four more layers: the stratosphere, mesosphere, thermosphere, and exosphere. At the exosphere, about 300 miles high, air thins out into outer space.

The higher layers of air don't play much of a part in the weather, but they do act as a protective shield for life on Earth. The stratosphere, for instance, holds the ozone layer, gases that absorb harmful ultraviolet light from the sun. The mesosphere, though thin, is still thick enough to burn up speeding meteorites.

The air is a mixture of nitrogen, oxygen, water vapor, and dust. Sunlight keeps the mixture afloat. Without the sun's heat, the air would collapse into a drift of frozen gases 20 feet deep.

THE SEASONS

Those of us who live away from the Equator divide our year into four seasons. They are spring, summer, autumn, and winter. Each season has its own kind of weather.

In North America certain kinds of weather are linked to the seasons. Spring in many places is windy and rainy, while summer may be hot and marked by afternoon thunderstorms. In northern areas a crisp, dry autumn might be followed by arctic blasts of frigid air.

Why does the weather change so dramatically through the year? The answer lies in the Earth's position in space. If you drew an imaginary line, called an axis, through the center of the Earth, you would see that the planet is tilted. When the North Pole points toward the sun, the northern half of the Earth—the Northern Hemisphere—gets more direct sunlight and has the long days and warm temperatures of summer. When the North Pole tilts away from the sun, the Northern Hemisphere, where we live, gets less direct sunlight and experiences the short days and cold temperatures of winter.

Watch the weather where you live. Do you see regular patterns in your seasons?

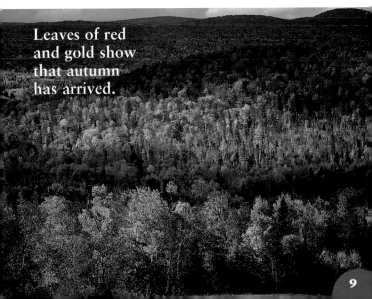

Leaves of red and gold show that autumn has arrived.

CURRENTS OF AIR AND WATER

Weather systems and sailing ships alike are driven by powerful winds that circle the Earth. These winds, known as prevailing winds and jet streams, are not the same as local breezes. Prevailing winds and jet streams are giant belts of wind that blow from the same direction around the world, all year-round.

Prevailing winds consist of polar easterlies, winds from the east, at each Pole; westerlies, winds from the west, across the middle of each hemisphere;

A jet stream looks like a river of clouds.

and trade winds just north and south of the Equator. Where the trade winds meet is an area of calm weather called the doldrums.

Jet streams are powerful currents of wind about 30,000 feet high in the atmosphere. They usually blow west to east. Jet planes flying east can hitch a ride on a jet stream to save fuel. Depending on air temperature, jet streams shift north or south, bringing weather systems with them.

The oceans have their own steady currents, as well. The Gulf Stream, which flows north along the east coast of North America and out to Europe, carries warm water—and winds—through the Atlantic. El Niño is a warm Pacific current that comes and goes regularly. El Niño can disrupt weather around the world.

READING A WEATHER MAP

Several times a day, meteorologists put together detailed weather maps of the Northern Hemisphere. The information for these maps comes from all over—and even above—the world. There are more than a thousand weather stations around the planet. Each one sends up weather balloons every day. These balloons carry instruments that read temperature, pressure, humidity, and wind speeds in the atmosphere. Meteorologists also collect information from satellites orbiting the Earth and from radar that measures wind speed and precipitation—rain and snow.

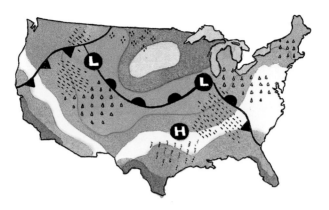

The maps used by meteorologists are detailed and complex, using hundreds of special symbols. Weather services also make simpler maps for the general public. These appear in newspapers and on television news programs. Simple weather maps show the leading edges of weather systems, called fronts, as lines with semicircles for a warm front, triangles for a cold front, or a mix of the two for a front that is not moving. Rain, snow, and ice may appear as raindrops, snowflakes, and slanted lines. High- and low-pressure areas will be shown with an H or an L.

Specific weather symbols appear in the "Forecast" entries of this book. Some are used only by meteorologists. Others may appear on your local weather maps.

TEMPERATURE

The first thing anyone wants to know about the weather is the temperature. Air temperature is the measurement of how much heat air holds. Heat sets air in motion. It is the engine that powers the weather.

FORECAST:
Numbers with a degree sign indicate air temperature. Winds from the north bring colder temperatures.

WHAT TO LOOK FOR:

✳ DESCRIPTION
Temperature is a measure of heat. You can check it on a thermometer.

✳ CAUSE
Almost all the heat on Earth comes from the sun.

✳ ACTION
January and February are the coldest months. August is the hottest.

✳ MORE
Temperatures in the United States are measured in degrees Fahrenheit.

Antarctica, at the South Pole, is the coldest place on Earth. Its yearly temperature averages -58°F.

HUMIDITY

You can't always see humidity, but you can feel it on your skin. Humidity is the amount of moisture, or water vapor, that is in the air. Warm air can hold more water vapor than cold air.

When water vapor cools, or condenses, near the ground, it turns into drops of water called dew.

○○○○○○○○○○○○○○○○
FIELD NOTES
When you breathe out into cold air, water vapor in your warm breath may condense into a tiny cloud.

FORECAST:
Two bars can mean light fog, which is often caused when warm, humid air moves into a cooler area.

WHAT TO LOOK FOR:

✳ **DESCRIPTION**
Moisture in the atmosphere can make the air look gray and misty.

✳ **CAUSE**
Water enters the air from oceans, lakes, and rivers.

✳ **ACTION**
All air holds moisture, but as it cools, the moisture sinks toward the ground.

✳ **MORE**
When humidity measures 100 percent, the air holds as much vapor as it can.

PRESSURE

An H and L on a weather map mark spinning masses of air called high- and low-pressure systems. Cool, high-pressure air sinks, pressing toward the ground. Warm, low-pressure air rises.

FORECAST:
An H or an L indicates a pressure system. High winds mean that high and low systems are close together.

WHAT TO LOOK FOR:

✳ DESCRIPTION
Pressure is the weight of air.

✳ CAUSE
Warm air rises and expands to create low-pressure areas. Cool air is heavier and sinks to create high pressure.

✳ ACTION
High-pressure air spins clockwise; low-pressure air spins counterclockwise.

✳ MORE
Pressure drops steadily as altitude, or height above the ground, increases.

FIELD NOTES

A barometer is an instrument that measures air pressure, usually in inches of mercury.

Crisp, blue skies and dry air arrive with high-pressure systems.

WARM FRONT

A front is just that—the front of a huge mass of moving air. A warm front is the leading edge of a chunk of warm air that is pushing into a chunk of colder air. Warm fronts can bring steady rain or snow.

FORECAST:
This symbol marks a warm front. High, thin, wispy clouds may be the first sign of approaching warm air.

WHAT TO LOOK FOR:

✳ DESCRIPTION
Warming air, thickening clouds, and precipitation make up warm fronts.

✳ CAUSE
Winds push warm air masses away from warm areas where they formed.

✳ ACTION
As warm fronts move in, they rise slowly, sliding up over colder air.

✳ MORE
Fronts were named after the military term meaning the leading edge of battle.

A slow, steady buildup of clouds means a warm front is moving through.

21

COLD FRONT

Like a schoolyard bully, a cold front that moves into warm air pushes it roughly up and out of the way. As the warm air rises, it often develops into violent storms.

FORECAST:
The symbol for a cold front indicates winds shifting toward the north and falling barometer readings.

WHAT TO LOOK FOR:

＊ DESCRIPTION
Strong, gusty winds and sudden storms signal a cold front.

＊ CAUSE
Winds push cold air masses in from the north or west.

＊ ACTION
A cold front shoves underneath warmer air, lifting it quickly upward.

＊ MORE
When a cold and a warm front meet and stall out, they create a stationary front.

Rainstorms develop quickly along a cold front.

WIND

On even the calmest day, a breeze touching your face will tell you air is in motion. At its most destructive, wind in storms can rip buildings from the ground.

FORECAST:
When you see this drawing, look for strong winds. Fast-moving clouds show that winds will soon be rising.

WHAT TO LOOK FOR:

✳ **DESCRIPTION**
Wind is simply moving air.

✳ **CAUSE**
Like pent-up air escaping from a highly inflated balloon, winds blow from high-pressure air masses to low-pressure ones.

✳ **ACTION**
Winds over uneven ground are turbulent. Over water they are steady.

✳ **MORE**
Alaska is the windiest state.

Strong winds, blowing at 32 miles an hour or more, can bend or break entire trees.

CLOUD

 A cloud is a floating collection of water droplets or ice crystals. It takes hundreds of millions of droplets or crystals to form one cloud. Clouds come in many types, each with its own name.

FORECAST:
Clouds, shown by a circle symbol, form when a cold front or a warm front begins to sweep into an area.

WHAT TO LOOK FOR:

* **DESCRIPTION**
A cloud can look like anything from a fluffy white puff to a flat gray sheet.

* **CAUSE**
Clouds form when air cools and water vapor condenses into droplets.

* **ACTION**
Clouds form anywhere from the ground to 12 miles up in the sky.

* **MORE**
Cloud droplets condense around tiny particles such as dust or salt in the air.

Water clouds have sharp, rounded edges. Ice clouds look fuzzier.

CIRRUS CLOUD

Cirrus (SIR-ehs) clouds are fair-weather friends. These delicate, high-flying clouds usually form in dry weather. Sometimes, though, they warn of an approaching storm.

Graceful cirrus clouds show that it will be a fine day to go to the beach.

FORECAST:
This figure represents cirrus clouds. They form in clear, dry air and also when a warm front is moving in.

WHAT TO LOOK FOR:

✳ **DESCRIPTION**
Cirrus are high, wispy, feathery clouds.

✳ **CAUSE**
Cirrus clouds are made of ice crystals. Wind pulls them into streaks.

✳ **ACTION**
Cirrus are the highest clouds. They form in the troposphere, three miles or higher above the Earth.

✳ **MORE**
Cirrus clouds will point in the direction of high-level winds.

FIELD NOTES
Cirrus clouds that have a flippy curve at their ends, like a horse's tail, are called mares' tails.

29

STRATUS CLOUD

 When the sky looks gray and flat and dreary, it's covered with stratus clouds. These smooth clouds may drop so low that they cover the tops of hills or tall buildings. Sometimes they bring rain.

FORECAST:
This figure indicates stratus clouds, which form when air is calm and moist. High ones may signal a warm front.

WHAT TO LOOK FOR:

✳ **DESCRIPTION**
Stratus clouds cover the sky in a gray sheet, usually blocking the sun.

✳ **CAUSE**
Water or ice crystals in calm, stable air form stratus clouds.

✳ **ACTION**
The base of a stratus cloud forms from ground level up to 6,500 feet.

✳ **MORE**
The word "stratus" means "layer" or "cover" in Latin.

Thick stratus clouds drop down to the water's edge.

CUMULUS CLOUD

Cumulus clouds can mean either fair weather or foul. Scattered cotton-puff clouds often mark a fine summer day. If they grow into towering, dark gray masses, they may bring rain or storms.

FIELD NOTES

Heat and water vapor from plants burning in wildfires can actually form clouds that produce rain.

The bulges in a cumulus cloud come from air currents rising and falling.

WHAT TO LOOK FOR:

✳ DESCRIPTION
Cumulus clouds are fluffy and round.

✳ CAUSE
The moisture in hot air that rises from the ground in columns condenses into cumulus clouds.

✳ ACTION
The cloud may start near the ground and climb to two or three miles.

✳ MORE
Cumulus means heaped. These clouds build upward, not sideways.

CUMULONIMBUS CLOUD

 Giants among clouds, cumulonimbuses are tall and dangerous. The violently swirling air inside a cumulonimbus breeds thunderstorms and tornadoes.

FORECAST:
A flat-topped figure stands for cumulonimbus clouds. Look for them on hot, humid afternoons.

WHAT TO LOOK FOR:

✳ **DESCRIPTION**
A cumulonimbus is a towering cumulus cloud with a flat base and top.

✳ **CAUSE**
These clouds form atop hot, moist air currents called convection cells.

✳ **ACTION**
Cumulonimbuses start near the ground and can top out at 70,000 feet.

✳ **MORE**
The biggest and most dangerous cumulonimbuses are called supercells.

The bottom of a cumulonimbus is made of water droplets, while ice crystals make up the top.

RAIN

 The sun's heat turns water into a gas, called water vapor. The vapor rises and clumps together in clouds. When the vapor cools, it turns into liquid water again and falls as precipitation—snow or rain.

FORECAST:
Droplets represent rain. Darkening skies, dropping air pressure, and increasing humidity come before rain.

WHAT TO LOOK FOR:

✳ DESCRIPTION
Rain ranges from a light drizzle to rain showers and heavy downpours.

✳ CAUSE
Melting ice crystals or condensing water droplets fall from clouds.

✳ ACTION
Tiny droplets inside a cloud collide and join together to form raindrops.

✳ MORE
The average raindrop falls at 14 miles an hour—the speed of a slow car.

Some rain showers can fall even while the sun shines. Showers last only a few minutes.

SNOW

Snow is not frozen rain. Each snowflake starts as a single tiny ice crystal in a cloud. Up to 50 other crystals may stick to it as it floats in the cloud. When a flake gets heavy enough, it falls to the ground.

More than 40 feet of snow can pile up each winter on high, cold mountaintops.

FORECAST:
Flakes stand for snow. Look for it when the temperature is near or below freezing and stratus clouds move in.

WHAT TO LOOK FOR:

✳ DESCRIPTION
Snow is made of six-sided ice crystals shaped like needles, columns, or stars.

✳ CAUSE
Snow forms when water droplets freeze into ice crystals inside cold clouds.

✳ ACTION
Snow can fall in brief flurries or for several days in storms called blizzards.

✳ MORE
Four inches of snow contains the same amount of water as 0.4 inches of rain.

FIELD NOTES
Chill dark paper in the freezer and catch flakes on it during a snowfall to study different snowflake shapes.

HAIL

 Pelting from the sky like tiny golf balls, hailstones come from thunderstorms. As hailstones grow inside clouds, they bounce up and down on drafts and add layers of ice until they are heavy enough to fall.

FORECAST:
This symbol represents hail, which begins as strong thunderstorms move in with gusty winds and heavy rain.

WHAT TO LOOK FOR:

✳ **DESCRIPTION**
Hailstones are lumpy balls of ice ranging from pea to grapefruit size.

✳ **CAUSE**
Hailstones take shape when water droplets collide and freeze together inside the cold upper parts of clouds.

✳ **ACTION**
Hailstones fall for a few minutes as severe thunderstorms move in.

✳ **MORE**
Hail can ruin crops and cars.

Hail comes in many
sizes. Larger stones
have spent more time
growing inside a
storm cloud.

FROST AND ICE

When the temperature dips below 32°F, moisture in the air can change directly into frost without being liquid water first. If rain is falling, it turns into ice that may coat your sidewalk.

Frost on low-growing leaves is a common sight in late autumn.

WHAT TO LOOK FOR:

❋ DESCRIPTION
Frost is made of feathery ice crystals. Ice from rain is usually clear or grainy.

❋ CAUSE
Ice forms from standing water or freezing rain. Frost occurs when moisture in air changes directly into ice.

❋ ACTION
It forms first in cool, low-lying areas.

❋ MORE
Frost crystals often grow on cold surfaces, such as windows.

FOG

Have you ever had your head in the clouds? You have if you've walked in fog. Fog is a cloud on the ground. Usually the sun will burn off fog by noon, but some valley fogs can last for days.

Valley fog is often seen in the mountains, where cool air rolls downhill at night.

FORECAST:
Bars represent fog. It forms
in low areas after clear, cool
nights and when warm, wet
air blows over cold ground.

WHAT TO LOOK FOR:

❋ DESCRIPTION
Fog is a thick, damp cloud that forms
at ground or sea level.

❋ CAUSE
Low, moist air that cools enough for its
water vapor to condense causes fog.

❋ ACTION
Fog usually forms in valleys, along
coasts, and over bodies of water.

❋ MORE
Fog makes it hard for people to see,
causing accidents along roads.

SMOG

 Smog is air pollution you can see. When cars and factories burn fuel, they release gases that stay in the air and irritate your lungs. Sunlight can react with pollution to create a hazy brown smog.

FORECAST:
This symbol for smoke represents air pollution. Smog is a brownish haze similar to smoke.

WHAT TO LOOK FOR:

✳ DESCRIPTION
Smog is hazy, brownish air filled with gritty particles and gases such as ozone, carbon dioxide, and sulfur dioxide.

✳ CAUSE
Smog contains fumes from factories and cars as well as volcanic ash, dust, and pollen.

✳ ACTION
It is thickest over cities and highways.

✳ MORE
Smog can sicken people and kill plants.

The main source of air pollution is the burning of fossil fuels—coal, oil, and gas—in factories and cars.

THUNDERSTORM

 The inside of a thundercloud is a violent place. Updrafts and downdrafts whip water drops and ice around at dizzying speeds. As drops and ice collide, lightning crackles, and thunder booms.

FORECAST:
This symbol marks a thunderstorm.Flat-topped cumulonimbuses and gusty winds mean one is coming.

WHAT TO LOOK FOR:

✴ **DESCRIPTION**
Heavy rain, strong winds, lightning, and thunder make up a thunderstorm.

✴ **CAUSE**
Warm, unstable air breeds these clouds. Strong drafts inside cumulonimbus clouds bring wind, rain, and lightning.

✴ **ACTION**
Thunderstorms are most common in spring and summer.

✴ **MORE**
Florida has more than 100 each year.

Thunderclouds may be sunlit on top, but they are always dark and threatening from below.

LIGHTNING

 Lightning is one of nature's most dramatic spectacles. One bolt of lightning can heat the air to 54,000°F, four times hotter than the sun's surface. Lightning strikes Earth up to a hundred times a second.

FORECAST:
A bent arrow represents lightning. Watch for thunderclouds. Lightning can strike before a storm.

WHAT TO LOOK FOR:

✳ DESCRIPTION
Lightning is a huge electrical spark made by a thunderstorm.

✳ CAUSE
It occurs when electrical charges build up in and around thunderclouds.

✳ ACTION
Lightning jumps within clouds, between them, or between clouds and the ground.

✳ MORE
Thunder is the sound air makes when it is heated by a lightning bolt.

Lightning usually strikes the tallest object in an area, such as a tree or a tall pole.

FIELD NOTES
Lightning striking sand can fuse it into branches of glass called fulgurites (FULL-gyu-rites).

SNOWSTORM

A big snowstorm, or blizzard, can drop several feet of snow in a day or two, closing schools and roads. When combined with stiff winds, a snowstorm is dangerous.

FORECAST:
Several flakes symbolize a snowstorm. Look for clouds, a falling barometer, and freezing temperatures.

WHAT TO LOOK FOR:

✳ DESCRIPTION
Snowstorms have heavy snowfall with gusty winds.

✳ CAUSE
Snowstorms occur in winter when a low-pressure system pulls together warm, moist air and cold, dry air.

✳ ACTION
Snowstorms often have rain on their south sides and snow on the north.

✳ MORE
Blizzards can last for several days.

Caught in a blizzard, this elk will have to scrape snow away to find grasses and twigs to eat.

ICE STORM

 After an ice storm, the world looks like a crystal palace. Yet ice brings danger. Roads and sidewalks become skating rinks and heavy branches fall from trees.

FORECAST:
This figure indicates an ice storm, which begins with dropping air pressure and rain falling into freezing air.

WHAT TO LOOK FOR:

✳ DESCRIPTION
The freezing rain of an ice storm coats cold surfaces with a layer of clear ice.

✳ CAUSE
Rain cools below freezing in frigid air, but stays liquid. Reaching a surface, it spreads and freezes instantly.

✳ ACTION
Ice storms can pull down tree limbs and power lines.

✳ MORE
Smooth, clear ice is called glaze ice.

The glittering spectacle of ice coating trees and bushes is lovely, but branches heavy with ice may snap off.

TORNADO

 Tornadoes are the most intense storms on Earth. With winds up to 300 miles an hour, they can cut a path of destruction a mile wide. If a tornado is coming, take cover in a basement or the center of a building.

FORECAST:
The tornado symbol is shaped a bit like the storm. Tornadoes grow inside severe thunderstorms.

WHAT TO LOOK FOR:

✳ DESCRIPTION
They are funnel-shaped columns of air that spiral down from cumulonimbuses.

✳ CAUSE
Warm updrafts and cold downdrafts inside powerful thunderstorms can set air spinning into tornadoes.

✳ ACTION
Tornadoes are most common in the south-central states.

✳ MORE
Tornadoes are also called twisters.

Kicking up dust and debris, the distinctive black funnel cloud of a tornado moves past houses in Kansas.

FIELD NOTES

Tornadoes are powerful storms. One in Ohio lifted cars of a freight train and hurled them 16 feet.

WATERSPOUT

 Waterspouts are small, weak relatives of tornadoes that form over warm coastal waters or lakes. They last 15 to 30 minutes and pack winds of less than 50 miles an hour.

FORECAST:
A waterspout symbol looks like a tornado over water. Watch for waterspouts on hot, still, humid days.

WHAT TO LOOK FOR:

✳ **DESCRIPTION**
Waterspouts are spinning columns of cloudy air that form over water.

✳ **CAUSE**
Warm water and moist, unstable air may lead to waterspouts.

✳ **ACTION**
Some waterspouts appear in groups of three or four together.

✳ **MORE**
Waterspouts are most common in the Florida Keys and Gulf of Mexico.

Unlike tornadoes, waterspouts often look clean and white.

FIELD NOTES

The water in a waterspout does not come from below, but from water in the cloud above it.

HURRICANE

 Monster of the weather world, a hurricane can be 500 miles wide and contain winds of more than 150 miles an hour. Its tall thunderclouds may drop more than 2.4 trillion gallons of rain a day.

FORECAST:
The symbol for a hurricane is a circle with wings. Look for hurricanes in summer when air pressure drops.

WHAT TO LOOK FOR:

✳ DESCRIPTION
A hurricane is a huge, spinning tropical storm with winds of at least 74 mph.

✳ CAUSE
Very warm ocean temperatures create groups of thunderstorms that are set spinning by trade winds.

✳ ACTION
Hurricanes are born in the tropics, the area north and south of the Equator.

✳ MORE
Pacific hurricanes are called typhoons.

An aerial photo of Hurricane Elena shows its central eye, an area of calm winds and clear skies.

FLOOD

Floods are usually a springtime disaster. Rain or snowmelt that swells a river over its banks can swallow land for miles. Floods can do great harm, but may bring relief from long dry periods, or droughts.

FIELD NOTES

Flash floods rise quickly when water runs off hard ground or is trapped between high walls.

River floods can cover tens of thousands of square miles, soaking farms and cities alike.

FORECAST:
This figure represents heavy rain, which can cause flooding. Sudden downpours cause floods in dry areas.

WHAT TO LOOK FOR:

✳ DESCRIPTION
A flood is composed of river or ocean water that overflows onto dry land.

✳ CAUSE
Heavy rain, melting snow, or storms cause floods.

✳ ACTION
Only two feet of moving water can float a car and knock you off your feet.

✳ MORE
Floods occur in low-lying areas near rivers, streams, canyons, and coasts.

DROUGHT

 You might think deserts have constant droughts, but dryness is normal there. A drought occurs when a place gets much less rain or snow than usual. Some droughts last for years.

FORECAST:
Weather maps might show a dust storm symbol during a drought, when wind kicks up dust from dry land.

WHAT TO LOOK FOR:

✳ DESCRIPTION
A drought is a long period that is much drier than normal for a particular area.

✳ CAUSE
Changes in large-scale weather patterns such as jet streams or ocean currents can cause droughts.

✳ ACTION
Long droughts may kill crops and allow topsoil to blow away.

✳ MORE
A short drought is called a dry spell.

A jigsaw pattern of cracked mud shows the effects of a drought in Florida's normally wet Everglades.

FIELD NOTES
Wildfires often follow droughts. Lightning starts a fire that quickly spreads through dry plants.

RAINBOW

 Ancient people believed that rainbows were sent by the gods. Scientists learned that they appear when sunlight bends through raindrops. Big raindrops produce the brightest, most beautiful bows.

FORECAST:
Light is split in a rainbow symbol. See rainbows early or late on a rainy day when the sun is behind you.

WHAT TO LOOK FOR:

✳ DESCRIPTION
A rainbow is a multicolored arc in the sky that appears when it is rainy and sunny at the same time.

✳ CAUSE
Raindrops split sunlight into colors and reflect them into a rainbow.

✳ ACTION
They rarely form in cold, dry winter air.

✳ MORE
The sun must be low in the sky and behind you when you see a rainbow.

In heavy rains, a rainbow may be shadowed by a secondary bow, in which the order of colors is reversed.

HALO

You may not notice them very often, but halos appear in the sky about once a week. A halo is a ghostly ring of light around the sun or moon that is the result of light shining through high, thin, icy clouds.

FORECAST:
A halo symbol shows a ring around the sun. To see a halo, watch for high, gauzy stratus clouds.

WHAT TO LOOK FOR:

✳ DESCRIPTION
Halos are circles of light that appear around the sun or moon.

✳ CAUSE
Halos are caused by light bending through ice crystals in the sky.

✳ ACTION
They occur year-round, but especially in winter and early spring.

✳ MORE
Remember to block out the sun with your hand if you're looking at halos.

Some halos have bright spots on either side that look like twin suns. These are called sun dogs.

FIELD NOTES
A sun pillar is another sky sight formed by light shining through high clouds that are thin and icy.

WEATHER-WATCHING

ARE YOU AN EXPERT weather-watcher? You can be! All you need to get started are your eyes, a notebook, and a few simple tools. Make your observations at the same time each day and write them down. See what patterns you can find. Here are five things to watch:

CLOUDS: Study the clouds and identify them using a field guide like this one.

Make a note of the direction in which the clouds are traveling.

WIND: Use clouds or a weather vane to check the direction of the wind. If the direction changes, it may mean a front is coming in with rain or snow.

TEMPERATURE: Check the temperature on an outdoor thermometer in the shade at the same time each day.

AIR PRESSURE: If you have a barometer at hand, write down the reading. Air pressure numbers also appear on the weather page in most newspapers. Is the pressure rising or falling from day to day?

RAIN: Collect rainwater in an open bottle outside. Put pebbles in the bottom to keep it upright. Measure the rain in a kitchen measuring cup.

NATURE'S FORECASTERS

LONG BEFORE people had satellites, they looked to nature for clues to tomorrow's weather. Much folklore and many sayings about the weather have been passed down to us. Some are true.

A RING AROUND THE MOON means rain, some people say—and they're right. These halos form when light shines through high stratus clouds, which often move in before rain clouds.

MORNING GLORIES are said to open up only when the weather will be bright. This

may not always be accurate, but it is true that some flowers are sensitive to light and will close on dark days.

PINECONES do open their scales in dry weather. Moist air makes them swell shut.

CRICKETS chirp more in warm, dry weather. They may even chirp louder as the temperature goes up.

FRIZZY HAIR can mean the weather is very humid. Human hair gets curlier when it is damp.

WHEN A GROUNDHOG sees its shadow on February 2, it does not mean that winter will last six more weeks. It just means February 2 is a sunny day.

U.S. WEATHER RECORDS

•**Highest temperature:** The hottest temperature ever recorded in the United States was 134°F at Death Valley, California, on July 10, 1913.

•**Greatest one-day temperature rise:** The temperature in Granville, North Dakota, rose from -33°F to +50°F in only 12 hours on January 21, 1918.

•**Lowest temperature:** On January 23, 1971, Prospect Creek, Alaska, recorded a temperature of -80°F.

•**Greatest yearly rainfall:** Mount Waialeale in Hawaii has an average rainfall of 460 inches. Rain falls there 350 days a year.

•**Highest wind:** The highest wind ever recorded on the Earth's surface was 231 miles an hour on Mount Washington, New Hampshire, on April 12, 1934.

• **Greatest snowfall in one day:** Silver Lake, Colorado, received at least 75 inches of snow between April 14 and 15, 1921.

• **Most destructive tornadoes:** In the "Super Outbreak" of April 3 and 4, 1974, 127 tornadoes tore through states from Alabama to Ohio. Six had winds of more than 261 miles an hour. Thousands of people were injured and 315 were killed.

• **Deadliest hurricane of the 20th century:** A hurricane hit Galveston, Texas, with little warning on September 8, 1900. More than 6,000 people were drowned in the 20-foot storm surge.

Death Valley, California, is the hottest spot in the United States.

GLOSSARY

air mass A large body of air with similar temperatures and humidity levels. Air masses can cover thousands of square miles.

air pressure The weight of the air pressing on the Earth.

atmosphere The layers of air that surround the Earth.

barometer An instrument that measures air pressure.

cirrus High-level, feathery clouds.

condensation The process by which water vapor changes into liquid water.

cumulonimbus Very tall cumulus clouds that bring rain and thunderstorms.

cumulus Low- to mid-level puffy clouds.

downdraft Cool, heavy air that drops down inside and below clouds.

Fahrenheit A scale for measuring heat in which the freezing point of water is 32 degrees.

front The boundary between air masses.

humidity The amount of water vapor in the air. Air that holds a lot of water vapor is called humid.

jet stream A narrow band of fast-moving air high in the atmosphere.

meteorologist A scientist who studies the weather.

pollution Dangerous chemicals and dirty particles that can harm the air and water.

precipitation Water that falls from the sky in the form of rain, snow, hail, or freezing rain.

stratus Low-level, sheetlike clouds.

updraft Warm air that moves upward, particularly under and inside clouds.

water vapor Water in the form of a gas.

INDEX OF
WEATHER

PHOTOGRAPHIC CREDITS
Photographs supplied by Animals Animals/Earth Scenes.

FIELD NOTES

FIELD NOTES

SKETCHES

FIELD NOTES

SKETCHES

FIELD NOTES

SKETCHES

FIELD NOTES

SKETCHES

FIELD NOTES

SKETCHES

FIELD NOTES

SKETCHES

FIELD NOTES